Haunted Houses
of the Hudson Valley
LYNDA LEE MACKEN

To all my Helpers, seen and unseen.

HAUNTED HOUSES OF THE HUDSON VALLEY

≈ ISBN 0-9755244-4-5 ❧

Cover design by Debra Tremper
Six Penny Graphics, Fredericksburg, VA

Cover photo of Wyndcliffe courtesy
of the Library of Congress.

Printed on recycled paper by
Sheridan Books, Ann Arbor, MI

CONTENTS

Introduction   1

Sunnyside   3

Huguenot Street Houses   7

Philipse Manor Hall   11

Abraham Kip House   15

Olde Rhinebeck Inn   17

Franz P. Roggen House   19

Cherry Hill   21

Beechwood   23

Lindenwald   25

U. S. Military Academy   29

Rokeby   33

Springwood   37

Dietz House   39

Merwin Cottage   40

Wyndcliffe   41

Church of St. Barnabas Rectory   45

Octagon House   47

New York State Capitol Building   51

Wilderstein   53

Wildmere Hotel   55

Estherwood   59

Bardavon Opera House   61

Bannerman's Castle   63

Highland Public Library   65

Delmar Hotel   66

Church of Christ Rectory   67

Lyndhurst   69

Ackley House   72

Acknowledgements   73

Bibliography   74

INTRODUCTION

Old houses and hauntings seem to go hand-in-hand. Since the Hudson River corridor was one of New York State's first regions to be settled there are many centuries old dwellings along the waterway and some of them are haunted.

What's more, the landscape of the Hudson Valley lends itself to the likelihood that ghosts exist... Native Americans storied the territory with mysterious legends. Early Dutch settlers imprinted the strange new landscape with scary fables. Washington Irving's writings enlivened the folklore and added more fuel to the already smoldering supernatural mix.

Where there's smoke there's fire, the saying goes, and surely there seems to be some truth to the spookiness as evidenced by the plethora of haunted houses.

There is a difference between ghosts and spirits. Ghosts are angry or confused beings who stay behind to exact revenge or don't realize they're dead; they're stuck in this dimension.

A spirit, on the other hand, is the energy of the individual that stays behind to tie up loose ends or simply because it wants to. Perhaps spirits desire to enlighten the living of life after death of the physical body.

The Hudson River vicinity captivated eccentrics, inventors, millionaires, mystics, idealists, and dreamers. As expected, the valley's paranormal populace is also unconventional. Typically the region's unearthly presences are subtle, much like the ethereal Hudson River School paintings where mists and fog shroud the scene – hinting at an otherworld.

The stories that follow fittingly start with Irving's Sunnyside, and then on to "America's oldest Main Street" in the Huguenot Street Historic District of New Paltz. This neighborhood showcases several stone houses built by French immigrants. Many spectral stories swirl about the early structures.

For centuries the shoreline of the Hudson River boasted an array of mansions owned by families whose names still resonate – Livingston, Armstrong, and Astor, to name a few. Many distinctive homes are now museums allowing the public a glimpse into the opulent lifestyles of America's aristocracy. The spirits who've stayed behind in some of the historic houses provide an amazing view into those earlier days as well.

Welcome to the haunted Hudson Valley where some ancient stone dwellings, church rectories, tourist hotels, military barracks, libraries, museums, mansions, and even a castle, claim a resident ghost... or two.

2

SUNNYSIDE
Tarrytown

Sunnyside is the former home of noted early American author Washington Irving. The historic house on 10 acres of grounds alongside the Hudson River is operated as a museum by Historic Hudson Valley.

Sunnyside contains a large collection of Irving's furnishings and possessions. Particularly of note are his personal accessories in the writer's study.

200 years before Irving possessed the property, Dutch-American Wolfert Acker inhabited the site. Known as "Wolfert's Roost," the property belonged to the Manor of Philipsburg; it consisted of a simple two-room cottage built in 1656. Irving even wrote a story about the place aptly titled "Wolfert's Roost."

At the time of Irving's purchase, one of the Van Tassels of *Legend of Sleepy Hollow* fame, lived in the small cottage. Irving's Sleepy Hollow legend is one of our nation's best-known ghost stories. He based his tale about the ghoulish rider on an actual apparition he heard about while serving as a tutor in Judge William Peter Van Ness' mansion[1] near Kinderhook.

---

[1] See "Lindenwald," page 25.

3

Washington Irving stays on at his charming estate.

Irving hired architects to improve the stone structure and transform the site into a little "nookery" – quaint and unpretentious. The result is today's easily recognizable wisteria-covered, stepped-gabled dwelling and Spanish tower.

Irving died in his Sunnyside bedroom on November 8, 1859. The Irving family continued to reside in the cottage until 1945 when John D. Rockefeller, Jr. purchased the house which opened to the public in 1947.

Gentlemen in top hats and ladies in hoop skirts welcome tourists to Sunnyside – a visit there is a journey into the past and into another world, literally. Not surprisingly, Irving's spirit now dwells in his treasured estate.

Irving's ghost, as well as those of his nieces who maintained the place for their uncle and resided in the home after Irving's demise, reportedly haunt the national landmark. The three-story tower known as the "Pagoda" is the author's favored haunt and his presence there is palpable. The phantom nieces are noted for their after hours tidying up.

Irving's nephew Pierre lived in the Tarrytown abode after his uncle's death and reported that one evening, as he sat in the living room with his two daughters, Irving's apparition walked right pass them, as plain as day, and entered his study.

The apparition of a headless woman walks the floors of the DuBois Fort.

HUGUENOT STREET HOUSES
New Paltz

Strolling along Huguenot Street is like stepping back in time. Celebrated as "America's oldest Main Street," the country road, amid a bustling college town, is home to four haunted houses.

In 1677, twelve Huguenots purchased 40,000 acres from the Esopus Indians and established "die Pfalz." Initially log huts went up but stone houses replaced them in 1692. The fact that they still stand is a testament to their construction and the effort to preserve them by the Huguenot Historical Society.

An excursion to the stone houses provides a view into existence three hundred years ago, and for some, a look into another sphere.

Initially constructed as a place of "retreat and safeguard," the 1705 DuBois Fort houses exhibitions, a gift shop, and phantoms from the past.

Mysterious sightings of a headless woman clothed in a brown dress shakes up staffers. Other inexplicable events, such as chairs moving and the unnerving feeling you're not alone, transpire in the ancient structure.

Is the specter carrying the ax in Abraham Hasbrouck's
house related to the woman without a head?

At the Locust Tree Inn, Abraham Elting's wife may
still reside at her mortal address.

At the Abraham Hasbrouck house, built in 1712, a male ghost clad in ancient garb and carrying an ax is witnessed. Could his hatchet somehow be related to the headless woman? It's a chilling thought. Theory suggests that ghosts abound on earth because their strong emotions keep them tethered here... we can only wonder.

A short walk down the storied street leads us to the Jean Hasbrouck House where yet another presence prevails. Elizabeth Hasbrouck lived in the house until her death in 1928 – well, she still does, kind of – only her form has changed.

A little further along, nestled among locust trees, stands a house built by Abraham Elting in 1759. Today's Locust Tree Inn is home to yet another female spirit.

Modernity caught up with the property in the 1970s when the house was converted to a restaurant and the surrounding farmland became a golf course. Ghosts don't take too well to change and will often react in some way to alterations in their environment. That's when the otherworldly occupant first materialized.

Employees tell of a female apparition at the inn whose olden form appears in their peripheral vision. Most surmise it's Abraham's wife who lingers at the site.

Caught in an other dimension, sometimes it's only Mrs. Elting's disembodied face that shows up or it's her mysterious footprints that she leaves behind in the newly vacuumed carpet.

PHILIPSE MANOR HALL
Yonkers

Philipse Manor Hall has long been the site of paranormal happenings. The eerie activity in the 300 year old residence has plagued staffers for years, particularly security personnel.

Those working the midnight shift were spooked by the murmur of imperceptible voices inside the empty building and foul odors floating through air. The sound of footsteps on the creaky staircase gave them goose bumps as did the tripping of motion-detectors when no one else was in the house.

After hours, neighbors often claimed they observed people moving inside the historic structure.

Not only is the house long on hauntings, it's long on history too.

In 1776, six months after the Declaration of Independence was signed, over two hundred Loyalists added their names to a "Declaration of Dependence." These colonial New Yorkers sealed their fate when they pledged allegiance to their sovereign, King George III of Great Britain.

At least one discarnate entity remains at Yonker's Philipse Manor Hall where strong emotions prevailed centuries ago.

Quite prominent among the signers was Frederick Philipse III, lord of the elegant mansion he used as a stopover on the long journey up and down the river between his home in New Amsterdam and the northern parts of his estate.

Unwilling to support the Revolutionary cause, Philipse was branded a traitor when he aligned himself with the British crown. Ultimately arrested on orders signed by George Washington, he received special permission to travel back to Yonkers to settle his affairs on the condition that he not aid the British.

In violation of his parole, he and his family fled to British-occupied New York City and later to Great Britain, leaving their estate behind.

Strangely enough, decades earlier during the wedding ceremony of young Mary Philipse, a Native American dressed in a crimson blanket suddenly appeared at the party and foretold the family's downfall. Indeed his dire prediction came to pass.

Following the Revolution, Philipse Manor Hall was sold at public auction, and occupied by various families throughout the 19th century until 1868 when the building became Yonkers' City Hall and remained such until 1908. Westchester County's oldest building that stands at Warburton Avenue and Dock Street has operated as a historic house museum sine 1912.

Frances Bennett is the founder of the New York Ghost Chapter (NYGC), an organization that conducts ghost "investigations." Bennett heard from a high-ranking Philipse Manor Hall staff member that an apparition of a man standing in front of a ballroom window was observed in broad daylight. The specter wore gold color pantaloons, a vest, and a ruffled shirt. The brown haired man stood gazing out at the environs. The woman wasn't scared at all, in fact, she described the experience as calming.

Bennett knew it was time to bring in her crew and the high tech gear. Technological progress is advancing the once baffling realm of the afterlife. Electromagnetic field detectors and other digital equipment now register anomalies previously out of range.

When the search was over the NYGC team's photos and videotapes contained orbs, which are balls of light commonly thought to be spirit energy.

Most chilling were the eerie remarks they recorded on audiotape. In response to the investigators' questions, voices saying, "we watch," and, "please go away" were among some of the mysterious answers they received.

When someone asked if they speak using their native tongue, the unseen entity responded in Italian with a lewd remark – "scata faccia," which translates to "s _ _ _ face!"

ABRAHAM KIP HOUSE
Rhinebeck

In 1703, five Dutch settlers from New Amsterdam (today's New York City) traded with Native Americans for the land that comprises modern day Rhinebeck. Among the five who swapped guns, powder horns, tools, blankets, and liquor, were Hendrick and Jacob Kip, for whom the community was first named "Kipsbergen."

The town's oldest house survives intact on Long Dock Road. Abraham Kip inherited the stone dwelling from his father and added a tavern room to the east end of the house for travelers. The present day living room served as the taproom back then.

Colonial taverns provided more than food, drink, and lodging. They functioned as gathering places where townspeople exchanged news and information with those traveling through the area. Sometimes the inns served as a refuge. Since the Kip House is built like a fortress that may well have been the case here.

The windows of the tavern room are wider on the inside than they are on the outside. This unusual design provided firing ports which made it easy to shoot out but prevented incoming bullets from reaching their mark.

When owners, Barbara and Eddie Fisch, worked in their backyard they likened their gardening to an archaeological dig. Pieces of blue willow pottery and a carved stone doll were among the artifacts they unearthed. In the attic, the couple found an old map that dated to the Civil War.

Some other relics from the past are the revenants that frequent the home they purchased in 1969.

The sightings began soon after the couple moved in. When witnessed, the ghosts appear dressed in 18th century garb, specifically riding breeches and boots.

Barbara, a former teacher and school administrator in Spackenkill, says the specters are harmless. The homeowner's first encounter gave her the distinct impression that the male phantom who stood in the hallway was observing to evaluate her.

The ethereal inhabitants keep a close watch on "their" house.

One time as Barbara installed Venetian blinds in her daughter's room she felt a tug on her dress. She turned, but no one was there. Deducing one of the spirits disapproved of the modern décor, she assured them verbally that the blinds were only temporary and would be removed once her daughter moved out.

Seemingly appeased, the spirit stopped yanking.

OLDE RHINEBECK INN
Rhinebeck

Another gently spirited Rhinebeck property is 340 Wurtemburg Road. Owned by Jonna Paolella and her husband Dave Kliphon since 1998, the Olde Rhinebeck Inn is an early American farmhouse beautifully transformed into a bed and breakfast inn.

Originally occupied by twelve generations of the Pultz family from 1738-1972, Jonna considers her occupancy there as steward for the historic property.

Four rooms are available for guests and in one particular chamber there's a baffling cabinet. When this room is rented Jonna advises the lodgers in advance that the closet door *will* open during their stay. The notorious door is securely latched, and not an easy one to undo, yet without fail the portal pops open.

A travel writer came to stay at the inn and of course the hosts sought to please. Nevertheless Jonna informed the guest of the wayward door. The woman seemed somewhat irked that she'd be sharing space with something intangible.

Before she settled down for the night, the writer set a chair in front of the closet door to thwart the inevitable.

The next morning the guest informed Jonna about her attempt to barricade the door. Apparently whoever, or whatever, stays in the closet felt irritated by the hindrance because during the night the French doors in the room blew open with a vengeance.

The Paolellas' genial spirit is dubbed "George," although the origin of his name is vague. He could be named after the second son of Johann Michael Pultz, the original homeowner.

The innkeepers and their guests also discern the distinct aroma of pipe tobacco floating through the house, especially in the living room. One can envision a long ago inhabitant relaxing by the fire along with his pipe. What's odd is that the smoke scent seems to contradict the laws of nature because it wafts down, not up!

Recently a wedding guest purposely placed his shoes by the hearth only to find them missing just moments later. He looked in "George's" closet and found the shoes neatly situated; his partner swore he didn't move them. The two men were visibly taken aback by the uncanny event.

The subtle presence at the Olde Rhinebeck Inn only enhances the cozy atmosphere. He's probably a Pultz family revenant who stays on at the place where he feels familiar, and welcome, just like all the guests fortunate to stay there.

FRANZ P. ROGGEN HOUSE
Kingston

Shortly after arriving in Kingston in 1750, Swiss immigrant Franz P. Roggen built his Dutch Colonial style house at the corner of John and Crown Streets in today's historic Stockade District. The property stands out from the city's other Dutch Colonials because of its ghostly reputation.

The British burned Kingston, New York State's first capital city, in 1777 because the town supported the American Revolution. The interior of the Roggen house was completely destroyed and remained in ruins until 1800.

During this time the house took on its eerie reputation. The beams that remained intact in the building were purportedly used as a gallows site.

When reconstructing the house the "hanging beams" were integrated into the restored structure. Thereafter, legend says, the spirits of those hanged from the rafters haunted the building.

(National Park Service photo by John E. Reinhardt).

It is rumored that the spirits of those hanged from the rafters used to rebuild Kingston's Roggen House stay behind at the historic structure.

CHERRY HILL
Albany

In 1787 Philip Van Rensselaer erected a 31-room Georgian mansion as the centerpiece of his 900-acre farm. For five generations the Van Rensselaer family inhabited the grand Cherry Hill estate, which still stands proudly at 523½ South Pearl Street, despite the fact that in 1963, the family sold the surrounding land and an urban neighborhood developed around the house.

Although the orchards no longer exist and the view from the stoop is of railroad yards, not farmyards, the house retains its dignity and elegance – and a presence from the past.

For many years, neighborhood residents reported a ghostly figure wandering the lower floor and walking on the terrace. The specter's identity remains a mystery to this day however.

The fact is that on May 7, 1827 migrant worker Jesse Strang murdered the Van Rensselaer's manager, John Whipple.

The prevailing tale is that ne'er-do-well Strang enjoyed an affair with Whipple's wife. She persuaded Jesse to kill her husband so that they could be together.

Strang purchased a pistol and shot Whipple through a window as the diligent and trustworthy manager sat with his employer going over accounts. Whipple died instantly.

Immediately apprehended, tried and convicted, Strang was sentenced to death by hanging and penned his confession, (a copy of which exists at Cherry Hill), before his died. Jesse Strang also retains notoriety as the last person to be publicly executed in New York State.

Mrs. Whipple served jail time as a partner in the crime.

The question remains — who is haunting Cherry Hill? Some say it's the convicted murderer. Perhaps his spirit is imprinted on the environment, caught in an endless loop, and continues to pace outside on the terrace waiting for a rendezvous with his lover, or for a clear shot at his victim.

More likely though, the restless wraith is John Whipple. Cut down by surprise in the prime of his life, it's likely his conscientious spirit stays behind to keep an eye on Van Rensselaer's estate.

BEECHWOOD
Briarcliff Manor

The majestic home called Beechwood, because of the property's bounty of beech trees, started out as a Colonial mansion originally built in 1790. The Midwestern Vanderlip family purchased the property in 1905 and expanded the dwelling in order to enhance the home with more lavish features such as a ballroom.

A gregarious couple, Frank and Narcissa Vanderlip loved hosting parties. Isadora Duncan danced on the lawn, the Wright Brothers landed a plane on the property, Annie Oakley shot up the place, and Franklin D. Roosevelt, John D. Rockefeller, and Henry Ford often visited.

Having derived his wealth from banking, Frank Vanderlip once served as Secretary of the Treasury. Service-oriented Narcissa and Eleanor Roosevelt were close friends and together they founded the League of Women Voters.

In the 1980s the historic mansion, which sits in a park-like setting overlooking the Hudson River, was renovated into three luxurious residences. Additionally, thirty-four townhouses went up on the property. The rolling lawns of the estate and the Vanderlip's formal gardens are still preserved. Many original landscape structures were restored including a small, stone gazebo with a moat. Today the romantic pergola is sometimes used as a backdrop for wedding ceremonies.

The tranquil setting belies the gruesome slaughter that occurred at the site decades ago.

Before the Vanderlip's tenancy, a religious fanatic known as "Mad Mathias" resided at the manse. The avant-garde character wore a heavy gold cross around his neck and his footman drove him about town in a chariot pulled by six white horses.

The story goes that he ritualistically murdered five beautiful virgins and buried them in the basement. When Mathias' butler found out that the young woman he loved was slaughtered, the killing spree stopped. The furious footman took justice into his own hands. He killed Mathias and buried him alongside his innocent victims.

Having no knowledge of the macabre events, Vanderlip servants often claimed to hear spectral footsteps running up the stairs and eerie gasping sounds.

While moving an armoire in the cellar, workers noticed an oddly plastered wall. An excavation revealed bones and a huge gold cross. The earthly remains were removed from the house and re-interred on the property – near the gazebo.

LINDENWALD
Kinderhook

Lindenwald is the name of the home and farm of Martin Van Buren, the eighth President of the United States. Van Buren descended from an old Dutch family and was born in Kinderhook in 1782. He served as a U. S. Senator, New York governor, Secretary of State, Vice-president, and became the first New Yorker to become President of the United States (1837-1841).

Van Buren ran two Presidential campaigns from the estate named after the American Linden trees lining the Albany to New York Post Road which runs right along the proporrty. This section remains unimproved to this day.

Van Buren, who wished to be remembered only as a "farmer," died at Lindenwald on July 24, 1862.

Today, Lindenwald is under the care of the National Park Service. The site provides a retrospective on the president's thirty years of public service and provides an astonishing insight into the past.

Originally built as a Dutch farmhouse by Judge William Peter Van Ness in 1797, some of the spectral activity inside the home is attributed to his insolent son,

Disembodied footsteps echo throughout Lindenwald.

John. An incorrigible gambler, John lost the property in a card game to Leonard Jerome. Although, not related to its haunted history, it bears mentioning that Jerome's daughter gave birth to Winston Churchill.

The sounds of disembodied footsteps and slamming doors throughout the house, reported by former residents, are attributed to son John's annoyance about losing the roof over his head.

Aaron Burr is New York State's most prolific ghost - his tormented specter shows up in many places all over the state including Kinderhook.

Burr evaded authorities by hiding out in the Van Ness estate after his fatal duel with Alexander Hamilton. A long-held tradition maintains that a rocking chair, a whittled wooden pig, and a faded calling card with the name "Aaron Burr" were found inside a secret room at Lindenwald. All this led to the legend that Burr hid out in the tiny space during his three year hiatus.

Whether he did or not, Burr's phantom did appear in the apple orchard; he wore a dark red coat and a lacy shirt.

Lindenwald's apple grove may be a magnet for the paranormal because a third wraith inhabited the fruit orchard. Not long after a dejected butler hung himself from one of the fruit trees, his eerie apparition dangled from the tree limb where be breathed his last breath.

The most delectable supernatural demonstration, and the one most often experienced at Lindenwald, is the aroma of pancakes sizzling on a buttered skillet on Sunday mornings. Could it be the estate's "Aunt Sarah" cooking up a stack of hot cakes from beyond the grave?

Free slaves toiled at the estate for many years. Aunt Sarah's legendary meals were surpassed only by her ability to rule her kitchen with an iron hand. Many in the house feel the presence of her spirit in the kitchen. Is it because she is unable to relinquish control of her earthly domain?

A hydrothermalgraph monitors the temperature and humidity inside the historic house museum and produces charts delineating the measurements for 24 hours. In *Ghost Investigator*, Linda Zimmerman noted that one New Year's Eve, the temperature spiked inside the dwelling as if warm-blooded individuals occupied the premises for several hours, even though the staff found no evidence, or possible entry, of any interlopers.

U. S. MILITARY ACADEMY
West Point

Located on a scenic Hudson River overlook, the United States Military Academy, commonly called West Point, was established in 1802.

During the Revolutionary War, George Washington headquartered at the site. Because the river was a central trade route, Washington considered the imposing plateau the young nation's single most important strategic location. He ordered an 150-ton iron chain drawn across the sharply angled Hudson in order to safeguard the vital waterway and prevent passage by the British.

West Point graduates, led by generals such as Grant, Lee, Sherman and Jackson, set high standards of military leadership during the Civil War for both the North and South. Eisenhower, MacArthur, Bradley, and Patton, were among an impressive array of Academy alumnae who met the challenges of leadership in World War II.

On the other hand, one-time cadets Edgar Allan Poe and James Whistler opted for alternative careers.

The Hudson River was a central trade route so George Washington considered the imposing plateau the nation's most strategic location during the Revolutionary War.

First inhabited in 1778, it is the oldest continuously occupied military post in the United States. With such a sweeping history there is little wonder why the austere institute harbors so many spirits.

Colonel Sylvanus Thayer, considered the "Father of the Military Academy," served as superintendent from 1817 to 1833. In his residence, it appears that his faithful Irish cook "Molly" has never left.

Legend says that when Molly died, a mysterious mark suddenly appeared on the kitchen breadboard – a message from the other side that her presence still lingered. Meddling with newly made beds by messing them up is another one of Molly's unearthly antics.

The son of a subsequent superintendent awoke one night and saw a woman in a long white dress standing over his bed. As he watched, she turned and drifted through the closed bedroom door.

There is an African American ghost who resides in the General's Quarters. This spectral soldier from the 1800s is a playful spirit who pilfers valuables such as wallets and jewelry and deposits them in the master bedroom. His antics create quite a disturbance for the commandant when distinguished guests find their money missing.

Such incidents caused the academy to contact psychic mediums in an effort to release the presence from the premises.

In the 1920s, servant girls living in West Point's Morrison House bolted from the general's residence screaming that a female phantom was chasing them. The woman who caused their terror was the dead wife of a professor who broke a promise to his dying wife and married her mother; the wife's unmitigated rage even reaches from beyond the grave.

The most documented case of paranormal activity happened in 1972, when several cadets witnessed the luminous apparition of a 1830s soldier. He wore an old-fashioned uniform consistent with that of a 19th century Cavalry fighter. The ghost, who sported a handlebar mustache, materialized in Room 4714 where he observed the modern day cadets studying and going about their duties. Satisfied with what he witnessed the out-of-place soldier turned crisply on his heels and stepped through the wall.

The cadets who shared the eerie event said that a rapid drop in temperature that turned the room icy cold preceded the specter's appearance.

Administrative officials took the sightings seriously since the academy's long-established honor code prohibits lying.

ROKEBY
Barrytown

Beginning as far back as the late 17th century, the Livingston family significantly impacted the development of the Hudson Valley. The family owned large tracts of land in today's Columbia and Dutchess Counties and west of the Hudson River in the Catskills.

Counting all the relations, as a family they constructed nearly forty riverfront homes between the towns of Hudson and Poughkeepsie which forms the majority of the 20-mile long Hudson River National Landmark District.

The most prominent member of the family, Chancellor Robert R. Livingston (1746-1813), helped draft the Declaration of Independence and negotiated the Louisiana Purchase. As a partner with Robert Fulton in 1807, he built America's first steamboat, the Clermont.

Livingston's sister, Alida, married General John Armstrong. Armstrong succeeded Chancellor Livingston as Thomas Jefferson's ambassador to France and served as James Madison's secretary of war during the War of 1812.

In 1815 the couple built their house initially called

(Photo courtesy of the Library of Congress. "Southwest front, looking northeast HABS NY 14-barto.v, 2-?")

Rokeby Mansion - where the spirit of a devoted servant still sweeps up the place.

La Bergerie after a flock of sheep given to them as a wedding gift by Napoleon.

One of the Armstrong's daughters, Margaret, married William B. Astor in 1818, son of John Jacob Astor, the wealthiest man in America at the time. Margaret named the estate Rokeby after a castle in the Scottish countryside depicted in a poem by the romantic poet Sir Walter Scott.

At the time, the children called their household slave and nanny "Old Black Jane."

Years passed and Jane's maternal responsibilities waned. Her demeanor began to change and she became fanatical about sweeping the floors. Morning, noon, and night Jane compulsively swept away.

One sad day, they found Jane's lifeless body with the broom still in her hands; she probably died of exhaustion. Supposedly the broom was buried alongside her body.

Each year on the anniversary of her death it's said that the brushing noise of Jane's broom is palpable in the grand house.

Astor family members occupied the estate for more than a century. One orphan kept crows at the house. In fact, there's a "Crow Room," painted and decorated with hundreds of crows. When his favorite one died, he claimed the bird came back and haunted the house. Séances were even held at the mansion in order to commune with the beloved pet.

Although a statue of Franklin Delano and Eleanor Roosevelt greets visitors, it's the president's willful mother, Sara, whose spirit stays behind at her beloved Springwood.

(National Park Service photos).

SPRINGWOOD
Hyde Park

Franklin Delano Roosevelt was born January 30, 1882 to James Roosevelt and his wife Sara Delano, both of prominent Hudson River Valley families. Franklin was their only child and they doted on him.

The idyllic setting of his youth was a quiet rural enclave. The wealthy family lived a country life among horses and cattle, hunting, fishing, iceboating, and riding on the grounds. Sara, a forceful character, proclaimed her affection for the place by declaring that they were "living life as it should be."

After James died in 1900, Sara and Franklin continued to live in the house. Even when he married Eleanor in 1905, the young couple lived with Sara.

Franklin's career required that the family live elsewhere for spells, but they returned to Springwood whenever possible. By 1944, ill and weary from the war effort, he said, "All that is within me cries out to go back to my home on the Hudson River."

Clearly Springwood possessed the family's heart, and given Sara's strong personality, it comes as no surprise that it's her indomitable ghost observed here on occasion.

Mabel Parker's presence haunted her Hudson abode.

DIETZ HOUSE
Hudson

The land that comprises the city of Hudson was purchased from the natives by Dutch settlers in 1662. New England whalers and merchants were drawn to the locale which grew rapidly as an active port. Hudson received its city charter in 1785 and the municipality came within one vote of being named the capital of New York State.

The city became notorious as a center of gambling and prostitution in the late 19th and first half of the 20th century. The racketeering came to an end in 1951 after raids of Hudson whorehouses by then Attorney General Thomas Dewey.

Beginning in 1904, citizen Mabel Parker lived in a 1830s neighborhood house for more than fifty years.

After her tenancy the Jay Dietz family resided in the house. Mabel apparently stayed put. Her spirit was consistently heard walking up the stairs then down the hall and into her former bedroom.

Whoever slept in the bed often complained that during the night an invisible someone tormented the occupant by removing the covers.

MERWIN COTTAGE
Kinderhook

A few miles southeast of Kinderhook stands a Dutch farmhouse "where Ichabod Crane lived." Called Merwin Cottage, today the property is owned by Broadway and television actress Esther Leeming Tuttle.

Martin Van Buren frequently visited owner Jesse Merwin, a local schoolmaster. The historical marker outside the premises implies that Merwin was the character Ichabod Crane in Washington Irving's *Legend of Sleepy Hollow*. Irving and Merwin were fishing buddies; a document, signed by Van Buren, certifies that Merwin was indeed Irving's inspiration.

In 1941 Esther, who prefers to be called "Faity," received warnings that the Dutch farmhouse she and her husband purchased as a summer home was haunted. Faity stated that the door to her mother-in-law's bedroom would inexplicably unlock and swing open of its own accord.

Once her grandson witnessed the apparition of a "white" woman on the porch. Some time later two Merwin sisters, past residents in the house, shared that their sister took her last breath on the front porch.

WYNDCLIFFE
Rhinecliff

Perched on a bluff high above the Hudson River stands the sad remains of a once imposing old manse called Wyndcliffe. Another Astor family member called this place home – a cousin – Elizabeth Schermerhorn Jones.

The name Wyndcliffe, and its Gothic appearance, are reminiscent of Wuthering Heights and its brooding tenant.   Almost predictably, this Hudson Valley mansion possesses similar parallels.

One of the most impressive homes in the country, Wyndcliffe boasted twenty-three rooms, boat and carriage houses, and terraced lawns. In fact, the grand 80-acre estate inspired the phrase "keeping up with the Joneses," yet this reputation could not enliven the imperturbable resident.

Ms. Jones lived alone at the red brick mansion after the death of her brother Edward in 1869. The story goes that once upon a time she fell in love but suffered the loss of her betrothed and wore black for the rest of her life.

Elizabeth endured a bout with tuberculosis as a child. Two of her siblings succumbed to the disease but her parents saved their daughter by shutting her away

(*Photo courtesy of the Library of Congress. "Uncorrected view of facades from southwest, distortion emphasized." HABS NY, 14-rhinb.v, 2-46.*)

Ghostly fox hunts, a little girl's specter, and the apparition of a hanged man all haunt eerie Wyndcliffe.

for nine months in the Mercer Street house the family owned in Lower Manhattan. They sealed the windows of her bedroom and kept the fireplace burning for warmth. These desperate measures secured their girl's survival into a hardy adulthood. Elizabeth ultimately matured into a steely old woman.

In 1852, she built her turreted villa and opened her door to notable visitors such as Henry and William James, as well as her niece, writer Edith Wharton, who often wrote of the mansion in her novels.

Despite the home's Gothic appearance, it's the carriage house that's haunted. Early on in the life of the country house a stable hand hung himself. Subsequent sightings of his ghost were reported.

The sound of a supernatural fox hunt plagues the property. Successive owners claimed they heard hounds barking and horses galloping through the woods. No such scenario existed – the strange noises were remnants of the past caught in the ethers and replayed on occasion.

Additionally, each Spring the specter of a little girl rolling a hoop with a stick played at Wyndcliffe. Might this be Elizabeth's young sister content to continue life as a spirit on the grounds of her sibling's great estate? Or perhaps it is the spirit of Elizabeth herself come back to haunt her home as she appeared in carefree and happy days.

Spirits stay behind and watch over the living at the
St. Barnabas rectory.

CHURCH OF ST. BARNABAS RECTORY
Irvington

Reverend John McVickar originally built the present day rectory as a summer house where he often entertained his friend, Washington Irving.

In 1854, his son William became St. Barnabas' first rector, when the parish church began.

Constructed from stone quarried on the former Rutter estate across from the church (the present location of Fieldpoint), prominent Irvington families, as well as the poor, worshipped in this holy spot.

For decades, the parish has provided inspiration and comfort to countless souls, but most importantly it's the kinship and acceptance. The same can be said about the invisible spirits who dwell within.

This rambling rectory on North Broadway is comprised of several clapboard additions. Since 1972, the charming structure has sheltered the rector, Reverend Dr. Charles Colwell, and his family — and at least two female specters.

One Colwell toddler witnessed an unknown woman sitting in a rocking chair near her bed calmly knitting. The apparition wasn't scary except that the child grew upset when the strange female didn't answer when she tried to speak with her.

When the girl grew up she discovered a photo in the rectory library of Isabel Rodgers Benjamin whose husband served as rector from 1867 to 1907. The youngster immediately recognized the dignified looking woman as the spectral lady who appeared in her room years before.

A short time later the rector's wife, Judith, fell asleep at the kitchen table while writing bills and awoke to see a woman's disembodied head — not Mrs. Benjamin's skull, but someone whose hair was styled in a bun. Mrs. Colwell felt that the incorporeal spirit telepathically conveyed to her the message that it was late and time for her to go to bed and get some rest.

Rev. Colwell sometimes finds the ghosts a bit pesky so he'll just admonish them to stop their annoying behavior. When a water faucet in the ground-floor bathroom mysteriously kept turning on full force the minister gave the unseen culprits a stern talking to and they've behaved ever since.

Those who perceive the spirits inside the handsome home concur that it's a feeling that they are being looked after and that heaven and earth are united in affection for eternity.

OCTAGON HOUSE
Irvington

The village of Irvington is home to a most unusual house. The lavish residence is an octagon-shaped house and is the only known eight-sided, domed structure in America.

Built in 1860 by banker Paul J. Armour, the property was remodeled and enlarged in 1872 by wealthy tea merchant, Joseph Stiner. Painted in shades of rose, blue, violet and red, the ornate home has been referred to as an "arrested carousel."

For some odd reason, even-sided octagon houses are prone to hauntings; Irvington's is no exception.

After Steiner's tenancy, a noble Frenchwoman and her daughter moved in. The beautiful girl immediately fell head over heels in love with a neighbor boy. The pair became inseparable but their love was ill-fated; the boy's parents previously picked out a more suitable woman for him to marry.

In spite of it all, the infatuated couple met in secret at every opportunity. When the coast was clear, the young woman crept up to the attic and placed a candle in the window as a signal.

When the Octagon House stood empty, people passing by often claimed they noticed a light in the attic window.

Ultimately, the steadfast couple planned to elope. On a gray, foggy morning they stealthily slipped from their houses. Under her cloak the girl wore the wedding gown she fervently worked on each night anticipating this special day. Her handsome sweetheart awaited her at the river's edge. Together they hurried to the dock and boarded the steamer.

Unbeknownst to the couple, the steamship was in a contest that day with its competitor. The vessel raced at full speed but the strain on the boiler caused the tank to blow. Many died instantly — among them, the young man. Other passengers drowned as a result of the explosion. The girl's pale, lifeless corpse showed up on the river bank the next day.

Her mother refused the body and without delay moved back to France. Passersby the empty house often claimed they noticed a light in the attic window...

Carl Carmer, chronicler of ghosts and legends, bought the odd-shaped house in 1946 and lived there for thirty years. He and his wife believed they lived with a spirit who often announced its presence with the palpable scent of cherry blossoms.

Once a year Carl's wife experienced a recurring dream. She dreamt that two women, one younger and one older stood outside the house embracing each other. The vision led Mrs. Carmer to believe that mother and daughter were happily reunited.

Two separate entities spooked the staff at the New York
State Capitol Building in Albany.

NEW YORK STATE CAPITOL BUILDING
Albany

The magnificent red-towered New York State Capitol boasts hundreds of arched windows and, unlike most capitol buildings, the structure is French Renaissance style and lacks the traditional dome.

Construction on the luxurious edifice, located at the State Street end of the Empire State Plaza, began in 1868 and was completed 30 years later for the then outrageous sum of $25 million.

Built in the tradition of great medieval cathedrals, many stone carvings grace the interior and are caricatures of famous politicians, writers, and some self-portraits of the carvers themselves. The centerpiece of the edifice is the magnificent "Million-Dollar Staircase," which took years to complete.

Governors Theodore Roosevelt, Franklin D. Roosevelt, and Nelson Rockefeller occupied offices in the building where they carried out official duties.

In March 1911, a raging fire erupted near the building's library. The conflagration took nearly twenty-four hours to extinguish and consumed half a million books and thousands of historical documents.

Most tragically was the loss of night watchman Samuel J. Abbott who perished in the blaze.

Some time after the inferno the sounds of moans, clanking keys, rattling doorknobs, and muffled voices became audible. Furtive shadows appeared and one employee felt a jolt of energy pass right through her as she encountered a misty gray blur hovering in a hallway.

Although psychics attribute the paranormal activity to Abbott, employees named their spectral entity "George." Some late night employees requested reassignment after encountering George's spine-chilling apparition roaming the fifth floor.

A night custodian once claimed that he observed his mop rise out of its bucket and begin to swab the floor as if worked by invisible hands.

Haunting activity in the building increases in the spring around the anniversary of Abbott's demise, which leads ghost hunters to believe that he is the one responsible for the eerie activity. However, prior to the deadly blaze another life was lost.

Laborer Cormack McWilliams fell from his scaffold as he worked overtime plastering a ceiling in the new capitol. Perhaps his specter is still on the clock and the one who scares staffers.

WILDERSTEIN
Rhinebeck

Built by the descendants of another one of Chancellor Livingston's sisters, Margaret Livingston Tillotson, Rhinebeck's Wilderstein Historic Site is the former home of the Suckley family. This five-story structure, designed in the Queen Anne style, was occupied by Margaret (Daisy) Suckley (1891-1991) her entire life.

Daisy was Franklin Roosevelt's cousin and close friend. She traveled extensively with FDR during his presidency, gave him his famous Black Scottie dog, Fala, and helped establish his presidential library.

When Roosevelt was fatally stricken at Warm Springs, Georgia in 1945, Daisy was at his side. After her death, the letters the pair exchanged during their friendship were discovered in the house under Daisy's bed. Their correspondence provides a unique window into Roosevelt's private life during his presidency.

Throughout her life Daisy acknowledged that an unidentified female ghost lived in the tower.

Wilderstein staffers say that as they pass Daisy's mother's room on the second floor, they often detect the scent of perfume or powder wafting through the air.

(Photo courtesy of the Library of Congress. South facade, looking northeast
HABS NY, 14-rhinb.v, 4-3.)

Historic Wilderstein where the resident spirit in the
tower kept its distance from the living.

WILDMERE HOTEL
Lake Minnewaska

The Minnewaska State Park Preserve is a 14,500 acre reserve located in the Shawangunk Mountain Ridge near New Paltz; it offers outstanding views of the nearby Catskill Mountains.

Originally part of Albert and Alfred Smiley's Mohonk Mountain House property, the Minnewaska Mountain House, or Cliff House, was built in 1879 overlooking the lake; a second hotel, Wildmere, soon followed.

Abandoned in 1972 due to exorbitant maintenance costs, the Cliff House burned to the ground in 1978. Wildmere closed in 1979 and burned down in 1986.

As with most old hotels the Wildmere held a ghost or two particularly in Room 444. The chamber stood at the far end of the hotel where unoccupied rooms were common due to persistent vacancies.

Among the hotel staff stories of paranormal activity ran the gamut from furniture being re-arranged in the fourth floor room to lights found on when they were definitely shut off, as well as doors found open when without question they were closed tight.

Supernatural guests stayed at the Wildmere Hotel on beautiful Lake Minnewaska in the Catskill Mountains.

Sam Lewit worked at the hotel from 1962 to 1978. He currently maintains the Lake Minnewaska website, www.lakeminnewaska.com.

During his tenure at the hotel he experienced the supernatural first hand.

On occasion he would hear the distinctive sound of a certain hotel room door open as he stood in a deserted hallway. Then he actually witnessed the door open and close as if by an invisible hand.

Sam's most vivid memory however is chilling.

One night in the dead of winter, when the hotel was closed, he strolled down the same hallway where the door mysteriously opened and shut. Sam thought he noticed the light on in the bathroom.

As he approached the room to check it out he observed a very old woman brushing her long grey hair. She faced away from the door, so he only saw her form from behind.

At that point, all alone in the furthest part of the huge vacant hotel, and looking at a ghost going about a post-mortem ritual, he did what any one would do – he practically flew down the stairs!

Estherwood – Westchester County's most haunted house.

ESTHERWOOD
Dobb's Ferry

The French Chateau known as "Estherwood" is a neo-renaissance mansion listed on the National Register of Historic Places. These days it is home to some of the Masters Schools' faculty members on its upper floors, while the first floor and grounds offer the perfect setting for parties and special programs.

Estherwood is also the most haunted house in Westchester County.

Inventor James Jennings McComb built the grand manor in 1895 for his young second wife, a local dark-haired beauty named Esther Mary Wood.

The happy couple and their three children from McComb's first marriage reveled in throwing gala musical soirées. At one party in particular Esther observed her husband present a female cello player with a nosegay of gardenias plucked from Esther's garden. Back then, this intimacy violated the marriage and implied more than a mere gift of flowers.

Heartbroken by the betrayal she bravely carried on tending to McCombs children day after day and crying herself to sleep night after night.

One sleepless evening in July, 1901, Esther found the program from that pivotal gathering while poking around her husband's desk drawer. Something scribbled on the program pushed her over the edge. That night Esther committed suicide by hanging herself with a silk cord from a balcony in the house – the crinkled program lay on the floor in McComb's study.

McComb fell into a deep depression and died in the manse a few years later.

The house stood empty until 1910 when Elizabeth Masters opened the building as a school for girls. Shortly thereafter Esther Wood's specter drifted down hallways and staircases causing mayhem among the students. Some overwrought girls left the school immediately.

Even locals observed the dead woman's apparition, particularly Hudson Valley resident Carl Carmer. The author witnessed Esther's nebulous form and described her black eyes as blank as she passed him by without notice. Carmer said that as her figure stoically climbed the property she stayed steely straight, her vaporous body at an "unnatural" slant going up the hill.

Recently, a young bride shared that a number of photos taken at her wedding reception held at Estherwood contained unexplainable orbs of light. One shot even captured the image of a woman in a mirror that's original to the 19th century estate.

BARDAVON OPERA HOUSE
Poughkeepsie

Originally constructed as the Collingwood Opera House in the 19th century, the performance hall on Market Street was transformed into a movie palace in 1923. Slated for demolition in 1976 protestors saved the historic theater from the wrecking ball. Today the Bardavon is the region's leading performing arts and cinema center.

Among the notables who've played this venerable venue are Mark Twain, Sarah Bernhardt, John Philip Sousa, the Barrymores, Martha Graham, Frank Sinatra, Milton Berle, Tommy Dorsey, Dizzy Gillespie, James Earl Jones, Harry Belafonte and many others.

Theaters are notorious for their resident ghosts and Poughkeepsie's Bardavon is no exception.

The 1869 opera house is home to Roger, a stage manager who was shot in the theater during its early years. According to Bardavon employees Roger has never left. In fact he's so much a part of theater lore that he has earned a spot on the theater's esplanade.

Roger's otherworldly antics include turning the water off and on, as well as the lights, which also blink in funny ways from time to time.

The spirit of a former stage manager carries on his duties
at the old movie house.

BANNERMAN'S CASTLE
Hudson River

The eerie ruins of Bannerman's Castle on Pollepel Island in the Hudson River are a gloomy vision, as you would expect with its four hundred year history as a haunted site.

Native Americans believed the tiny island swarmed with ghosts. Early Europeans thought goblins possessed the land and controlled the difficult river passage where fierce currents, and unpredictable storms and winds could capsize their boats. To test their mettle, sailors making their first journey up the river were left at the island until the ship returned.

Scotland native Francis Bannerman inherited his father's military surplus business in New York City. After the Spanish-American War he bought up U. S. Army excess equipment, including millions of rounds of ammunition. In 1900 he purchased Pollepel Island as a storage facility since his Manhattan storeroom couldn't contain his enormous cache.

Bannerman's wife believed she lived as a Queen of England in a previous lifetime so the arms dealer set about to single-handedly design a residence in the style of an Old World castle where she would feel at home and he could satisfy his own ancestral leaning. In true fashion the plan included a moat, drawbridge, hidden tunnels, and a dungeon.

In order to build docks, Bannerman bought old ships, sunk them and covered them with concrete.

A tugboat captain, particularly fond of his craft, asked workers to wait until he went downriver before they sunk his much-loved craft. Tactlessly, the ship went down before he could even turn away. Furious with their lack of consideration, the hapless captain cursed the crew and Bannerman too, ominously swearing his return.

A lodge went up over the drowned tug and for years workers heard the distinctive double ring of a ship's bell – the signal that a boat is going in reverse. All believed the ethereal ringing was the captain's angry spirit eternally backing his boat away from the island.

Apparitions of headless soldiers were widespread on the island in Bannerman's day. Were these specters the victims of some of the weapons amassed at the site?

Once during a routine test-fire a shell accidentally fell off the mountain and through the roof of one of the warehouses. An explosion ensued destroying the building as well as the unfortunate workers inside. Supposedly their ghosts also haunted the island.

HIGHLAND PUBLIC LIBRARY
Highland

The Highland Public Library is housed in the former home of Dr. Caspar Ganse and his wife, Georgianna. The couple was the sole owners of the property where the doctor practiced dentistry. Childless, they bequeathed the house and the remains of their estate to their charitable foundation.

The library evolved from a reading room formed during the Women's Suffrage movement in 1915.

Librarian Sara Ottaviano shared that doors slam inexplicably disturbing the hushed atmosphere and window blinds open on their own. Books mysteriously fall from shelves and once a quarter appeared out of the blue and rolled along the floor.

Most attribute the perplexing activity to Georgianna's spirit. One passerby even sighted a female apparition in the attic window after hours.

Some suggest it could be artist Lilian Spencer however. According to town historian, Terry Scott, the local artist bartered some of her paintings for dental services during financial hardship. One of her canvasses still hangs in the library office.

DELMAR HOTEL
Ellenville

Ellenville's Delmar Hotel no longer exists, but when it operated as a popular hostel its eerie hauntings were famous.

Weary travelers described one of the phantoms as a rotund black man. Although harmless, it was nevertheless disconcerting to see the strange, dark shape emerge from the corner of the room and slowly manifest into the solid image of a "football linebacker." The onerous apparition frequently made trips back and forth to the bathroom. On each occasion the specter spent time at the sink in the room after his trips to the toilet.

One traumatized hiker said that he observed the ghost's head detach from its body. Then the decapitated head stayed at the foot of the bed while its headless form approached the prone young man. The guy started screaming – frightfully so. His shrieks scared the ghoul into the bathroom.

Another entity sometimes appeared outside in the parking lot. Every now and then summertime guests observed the specter of a little girl bouncing a ball.

CHURCH OF CHRIST RECTORY
Poughkeepsie

The late Episcopalian Bishop James A. Pike was a devoted supporter of spiritualism, the belief in communication with the dead. For that reason, it's no surprise that Pike encountered the paranormal when he served as rector of the Church of Christ in Poughkeepsie.

In 1966, Pike's 20-year-old son shot himself in a New York City hotel room. Spirit medium Arthur Ford asserted he'd been contacted by the bishop's deceased son Jim. Pike even wrote a book about the personal evidence that Ford offered him to prove the contact, and other instances of "proof" the bishop experienced.

Pike took over the Poughkeepsie post from the previous rector who diametrically opposed Pike's progressive ideas. When the controversial cleric became rector at the Church of Christ strange things started to happen.

Altar candles blew out during his services, doors slammed, and overhead objects appeared to move although in reality they did not. When Pike recognized the previous rector's specter walking up the stairs to the bell tower, he strongly suspected that the deceased reverend was to blame for the inexplicable goings on at the church.

One eerie event was observed by the entire congregation. As Bishop Pike conducted a church service a bat flew out of nowhere and began to assail the cleric. By the time he reached for something to defend himself, the spectral bat vanished as quickly as it appeared. Since Pike noticed the dead rector's ghost near the altar on occasion, he attributed this assault to his predecessor as well.

Another otherworldly tale at the site involves a parishioner who fell asleep on a pew as her sister practiced the organ. The woman awoke to a ghoulish face laughing at her.

Nothing uncanny has transpired at the historic house of worship in quite some time. Perhaps the clashing bishops rectified their differences in the great beyond.

LYNDHURST
Tarrytown

Lyndhurst is a Gothic Revival country house that sits on 67 acres alongside the Hudson River just south of the Tappan Zee Bridge on US Route 9.

Designed in 1838, the romantic structure was first home to former New York City Mayor William Paulding, then merchant George Merritt, and finally the Gould family headed by railroad tycoon Jay Gould. Gould's daughter donated the prime parcel to the National Trust for Historic Preservation in 1961.

Open to the public, the asymmetrical building earned the nickname "Paulding's Folly" because of its fantastically unusual design. The exterior limestone was quarried at Sing Sing (now Ossining).

The charming, turreted mansion, unlike others along the Hudson, contains few rooms, has narrow hallways and sharply arched windows, which add to its somber appeal.

The house is adjacent to Washington Irving's Sunnyside and its setting is a naturalistic park with rolling lawns and a curving entrance drive that reveals astonishing views.

Lyndhurst – not your traditional haunted house.

The property served as the set location for the Collinwood Estate in the two *Dark Shadows* movies in the 1970s. The mansion grounds provided many backdrops in both films as well as the television program of the same name. Scenes shot here were enhanced by fog machines that created an eerie atmosphere.

Lyndhurst is not haunted in the traditional sense but there is clearly another dimension to the historic property.

A prominent architect took thousands of photographs of the beautiful estate over the course of his lifetime. Dozens revealed unexplainable anomalies according to Monica Randall in *Phantoms of the Hudson Valley*. "Bursts of blue light" appear in many shots of the unused rooms. 21st century "ghost hunters" contend that these unusual light forms are the essence of spirits manifesting in our mortal world.

Cameras are known to sometimes capture sights unseen by the naked eye. The most dramatic picture developed when the perfectly manicured lawn was photographed. One resulting photo shows a lake with a castle positioned in the background.

Subsequent research revealed that decades ago a pond did indeed exist on that spot.

ACKLEY HOUSE
Nyack

One Laveta Place is a bona fide haunted house according to the New York State Supreme Court.

The Hudson River property squabble turned out to be a landmark case that determined if a house is known to be haunted that information must be divulged in any real estate transaction as a pre-existing condition.

In 1990 prospective buyers made a down payment on the Ackley house. When a local architect casually mentioned haunting activity in the house, the buyers wanted out of the deal. The prospect of sharing space with specters was too much to bear for the potential buyers; they wanted their deposit back.

The purchasers found out that the owner willingly shared the story of the spirits who occupied her home with *Reader's Digest*. The local ghost tour operator also featured the house as a stop on the itinerary.

Mrs. Ackley refused to void the contract. The case went all the way to the State Supreme Court. The judge ruled in favor of the buyers because Ackley actively promoted her house as haunted, but when it came to selling, she failed to disclose the information.

ACKNOWLEDGMENTS

I'd like to express my appreciation to the following individuals for their cheerful assistance: Shelley Glick, Reference Librarian, Briarcliff Manor Library; Heather Iannucci, Site Manager, Philipse Manor Hall, who supplied inaccessible articles; Sam Lewit, former staffer at the now defunct Wildmere Hotel, Lake Minnewaska; Sara Ottaviano, Highland Public Library; Jonna Paolella, co-owner of the Olde Rhinebeck Inn, for sharing her stories; Cynthia Owen Philip, historian and author, who went out of her way to check on Wyndcliffe's ruins; and Sandy Bartlett, Librarian, Morton Memorial Library, Rhinebeck.

Heartfelt thanks to Debbie Devrous, Phyllis Sabia, and Melissa Wade for their editing skills.

Thank you, Daniel Sabia, for driving to West Point!

My gratitude also goes to Graphic Designer, Debra Tremper who creates the covers for Black Cat Press titles. Deb is artistic, patient, pleasant, and talented. Check out her website: www.sixpennygraphics.com.

BIBLIOGRAPHY

Allison, Rev. Charles Elmer. *The History of Yonkers.* Harbor Hill Books, 1984.

Bigg, Nick. "Tales from Merwin." *Columbia County History & Heritage;* Fall 2002.

Dominguez, Robert. "Spirit Catchers." *New York Daily News;* October 20, 2002.

Favicchio, Donna. "Valley of the Spirits." *Highland Mid-Hudson Post;* October 28, 2004.

Hauck, Dennis William. *The National Directory of Haunted Places.* Penguin Press; 1996.

Holzer, Hans. *Travel Guide to Haunted Houses.* Black Dog & Leventhal Publishers; 1998.

Macken, Lynda Lee. *Empire Ghosts.* Black Cat Press; 2004.

Matthews, Kathryn. "This Old House Has Ghosts." *New York Times,* October 13, 2006.

Pitkin, David J. *Ghosts of the Northeast.* Aurora Publications; 2002.

Randall, Monica. *Phantoms of the Hudson Valley.* Overlook Press, 1995.

Revai, Cheri. *Haunted New York.* Stackpole Books; 2005.

Sandiford, Frances. "A Spirit Named George." www.abouttownguide.com.

Smitten, Susan. *Ghost Stories of New York State.* Lone Pine Publishing, Inc.; 2004.

Zimmerman, Linda. *Ghost Investigator.* Spirited Books; 2002.

WEBSITES

Bardavon 1869 Opera House: www.bardavon.org
Ghosts of the Hudson Valley: www.bearsystems.com
Highland Public Library: www.highlandlibrary.org
Historic Hudson Valley: www.hudsonvalley.org
Huguenot Historical Society: www.huguenotstreet.org
Hudson Valley Ruins: www.hudsonvalleyruins.org
Lake Minnewaska: www.lakeminnewaska.org
National Park Service: www.nps.gov
Olde Rhinebeck Inn: www.rhinebeckinn.com
St Barnabas Church: www.stbarnabaschurch.org
Wilderstein Historic Site: www.wilderstein.org

Bannerman's Castle on Pollepel Island in the Hudson River.